Answer the Phone

by Lelia Mander

BLACKBIRCH®
PRESS

THOMSON

GALE

San Diego • Detroit • New York • San Francisco • Cleveland • New Haven, Conn. • Waterville, Maine • London • Munich

For more information, contact
The Gale Group, Inc.
27500 Drake Rd.
Farmington Hills, MI 48331-3535
Or you can visit our Internet site at http://www.gale.com

Photo Credits: see page 47.

LIBRARY OF CONGRESS CATALOGING-IN-PUBLICATION DATA

Mander, Lelia.
  Answer the telephone / by Lelia Mander.
    p. cm. — (Step back science series)
  Summary: Explains how telephones work and discusses the   emergency number 911.
  Includes bibliographical references and index.
  ISBN 1-56711-682-5 (hardback)
  1. Telephone—Juvenile literature.   [1. Telephone.] I. Title.

  II. Series.
  TK6165.M36 2003
  621.385—dc21   2002011728

Contents

Answer the Phone

How to Use This Book

Each Step Back Science book traces the path of a science-based act backwards, from its result to its beginning.

Each double-page spread like the ones below explains one step in the process.

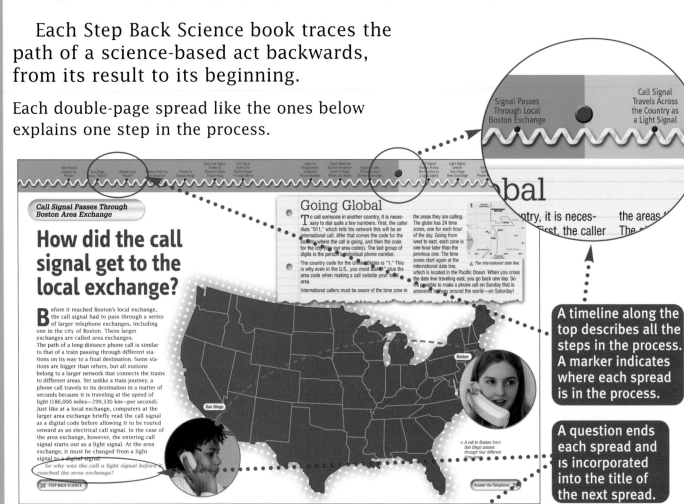

Call Signal Passes Through Boston Area Exchange

How did the call signal get to the local exchange?

Before it reached Boston's local exchange, the call signal had to pass through a series of larger telephone exchanges, including one in the city of Boston. These larger exchanges are called area exchanges. The path of a long-distance phone call is similar to that of a train passing through different stations on its way to a final destination. Some stations are bigger than others, but all stations belong to a larger network that connects the trains to different areas. Yet unlike a train journey, a phone call travels to its destination in a matter of seconds because it is traveling at the speed of light (186,000 miles—299,330 km—per second). Just like at a local exchange, computers at the larger area exchange briefly read the call signal as a digital code before allowing it to be routed onward as an electrical call signal. In the case of the area exchange, however, the entering call signal starts out as a light signal. At the area exchange, it must be changed from a light signal to a digital signal.

So why was the call a light signal before it reached the area exchange?

28 STEP BACK SCIENCE

Going Global

To call someone in another country, it is necessary to dial quite a few numbers. First, the caller dials "011," which tells the network this will be an international call. After that comes the code for the country where the call is going, and then the code for the city (like our area codes). The last group of digits is the person's individual phone number.

The country code for the United States is "1." This is why even in the U.S., you must dial "1" plus the area code when making a call outside your local area.

International callers must be aware of the time zone in the areas they are calling. The globe has 24 time zones, one for each hour of the day. Going from west to east, each zone is one hour later than the previous one. The time zones start again at the international date line, which is located in the Pacific Ocean. When you cross the date line traveling east, you go back one day. So it is possible to make a phone call on Sunday that is answered halfway around the world—on Saturday!

▲ *The international date line.*

Boston

San Diego

◄ *A call to Boston from San Diego passes through four different time zones.*

Answer the Telephone 29

A timeline along the top describes all the steps in the process. A marker indicates where each spread is in the process.

A question ends each spread and is incorporated into the title of the next spread.

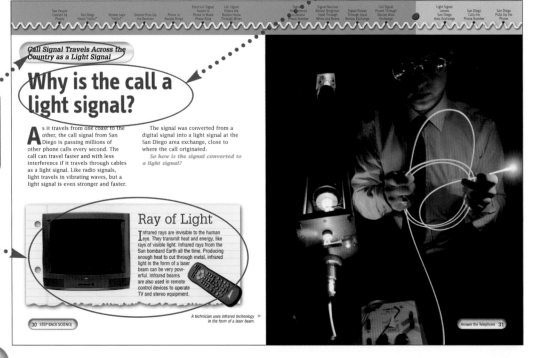

Call Signal Travels Across the Country as a Light Signal

Why is the call a light signal?

As it travels from one coast to the other, the call signal from San Diego is passing millions of other phone calls every second. The call can travel faster and with less interference if it travels through cables as a light signal. Like radio signals, light travels in vibrating waves, but a light signal is even stronger and faster.

The signal was converted from a digital signal into a light signal at the San Diego area exchange, close to where the call originated.
So how is the signal converted to a light signal?

A short description gives a quick answer to the question asked at the end of the previous step.

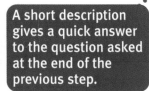

Sidebars show interesting related information.

Ray of Light

Infrared rays are invisible to the human eye. They transmit heat and energy, like rays of visible light. Infrared rays from the Sun bombard Earth all the time. Producing enough heat to cut through metal, infrared light in the form of a laser beam can be very powerful. Infrared beams are also used in remote control devices to operate TV and stereo equipment.

30 STEP BACK SCIENCE

A technician uses infrared technology ▶ in the form of a laser beam.

Answer the Telephone 31

Side Step spreads, like the one below, offer
separate but related information.

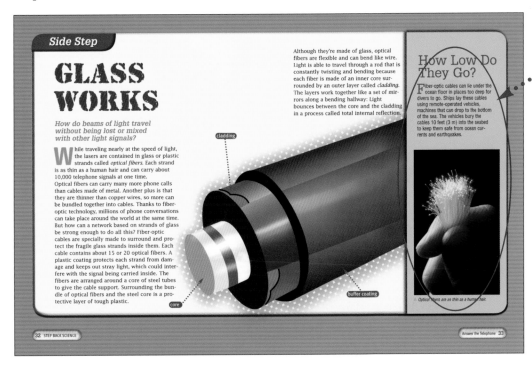

The Big Picture, on pages 40-41, shows
the entire process at a glance.

San Diego
Hears "Hello?"

Boston Says
"Hello?"

Boston Picks Up
the Receiver

Phone in
Boston Rings

Electrical Signal
Travels to
Phone to Make
Phone Ring

Call Signal
Enters the
Boston Home
Through Wires

Two People Connect by Phone

How does a telephone work to connect people?

A person in Boston, Massachusetts, answers the phone when it rings. The caller is a friend in San Diego, California. More than 2,700 miles (4,345 km) separate the two people, but all the caller had to do is pick up the telephone and call the Boston phone number. A connection is made—and the act is completed—when the answerer picks up the phone and says, "Hello?" and the caller replies, "Hi!"

Sounds simple, but that is really where the mystery begins.

How can the caller hear the answerer's voice?

Signal is Programmed as Boston Phone Number

Signal Reaches Boston Neighbor-hood Through Wires and Boxes

Signal Passes Through Local Boston Exchange

Call Signal Passes Through Boston Area Exchange

Call Signal Travels Across the Country as a Light Signal

Light Signal Leaves San Diego Area Exchange

San Diego Calls the Phone Number

San Diego Picks Up the Phone

Two People Connect by Phone

Boston Says "Hello?"

Boston Picks Up the Receiver

Phone in Boston Rings

Electrical Signal Travels to Phone to Make Phone Ring

Call Signal Enters the Boston Home Through Wires

San Diego Hears "Hello?"

How can San Diego hear the answerer's voice?

The spoken word has been converted from sound waves into an electrical signal that travels through wires to San Diego. San Diego can hear "Hello" because the phone's earpiece receives electrical signals and converts them back into sound waves. This change is necessary because, although the answerer speaks into the phone and produces the invisible sound waves, only electrical signals can travel through the phone wires.

Here is how the earpiece makes that conversion: When the electrical signal reaches the San Diego phone, it travels to a wire that is wound around a coil inside the earpiece. There, the signal creates a weak magnetic field. Right behind the coil is a magnet, which responds to this magnetic pull by vibrating as it attracts and repels from the coil. These vibrations squeeze and stretch the air around a thin, metal disc called a *diaphragm*.

The diaphragm's movement creates sound waves that come through the earpiece and are very similar to the sound waves that originally came from the answerer's voice.

But how is the electrical signal that comes through the phone created?

A Phone Is Born – By Accident

On June 2, 1875, Alexander Graham Bell and his assistant, Thomas Watson, were working on a new kind of telegraph — an instrument that sent messages in the form of electrical codes. Their version used steel reeds to create vibrations in the transmitter and receiver. When Watson plucked a reed on the transmitting end, Bell heard a twanging sound on the receiver in the next room. Bell thought that if a transmitter could send this sound to a receiver over a wire,

it could send the similar sound of a human voice. He soon discovered that a wire resting in a conducting liquid and vibrated by a voice could be made to produce a vibrating current. In other words, he had been right: Speech could be transmitted over wire.

On March 10, 1876, Bell knocked over the battery acid he was testing as a conducting liquid. Upset, Bell supposedly yelled, "Mr. Watson, come here. I want you!" Next door, Watson heard Bell's voice through the wire. He had received the first telephone call.

Signal is Programmed as Boston Phone Number

Signal Reaches Boston Neighborhood Through Wires and Boxes

Signal Passes Through Local Boston Exchange

Call Signal Passes Through Boston Area Exchange

Call Signal Travels Across the Country as a Light Signal

Light Signal Leaves San Diego Area Exchange

San Diego Calls the Phone Number

San Diego Picks Up the Phone

Parts of a phone

Inside the *mouthpiece* of a receiver, sound waves are turned into an electrical signal that can travel through the phone and its connected wires.

The *earpiece* of a receiver turns an electrical signal back into sound waves, so people can understand each other while on the phone.

A telephone has an on/off switch called the *hook switch*. It is released when someone picks up the receiver.

Phone numbers are pressed on the *keypad*, which is electronically connected to the phone and its wires.

The *ringer* is a device inside the phone that rings to announce a call.

The telephone is connected to an electrical outlet, or *telephone jack*, by a wire. An electrical signal travels from the phone through this wire beyond the jack to a vast network of wires, cables, and computers that link phones all over the world.

earpiece

To strengthen and direct sound waves so people can hear each other clearly, earpieces are designed to be slightly concave, or bowl-shaped.

keypad

mouthpiece

telephone wire

Two People
Connect by
Phone

San Diego
Hears "Hello?"

Boston Picks Up
the Receiver

Phone in
Boston Rings

Electrical Signal
Travels to
Phone to Make
Phone Ring

Call Signal
Enters the
Boston Home
Through Wires

Boston Says "Hello?"

How is the electrical signal that comes through the phone created?

As the person in Boston speaks, the sound waves that are created enter the mouthpiece. Wires and coils change the waves into an electrical signal. The mouthpiece works in a way similar to the earpiece. When sound waves go into the mouthpiece, a diaphragm—which has a current of electricity from the local telephone company flowing through it—vibrates. Its movement causes a wire coil and magnet inside the mouthpiece to change the waves to electrical signals.

Since an electrical signal can travel over wires at about two-thirds the speed of light, all of this happens incredibly fast. It is so fast, in fact, that the caller connects with the answerer and hears a greeting as it is spoken. To start this process, all the answerer had to do was pick up the receiver when the phone rang.

So what happens when the answerer picks up the phone's receiver?

diaphragm

Carbon Copies

Mouthpieces in early telephones used thousands of tiny particles of carbon to pick up the diaphragm's vibrations. Sound waves would vibrate the diaphragm, which would then press against the carbon particles. Carbon is an element that carries a small amount of electricity. So when the carbon granules were pressed together, electricity could pass more easily among the granules and build strength. This created the electrical signal needed to send sound through the telephone network.

A "coffin phone" from the 1870's

Two People Connect by Phone

San Diego Hears "Hello?"

Boston says "Hello?"

Phone in Boston Rings

Electrical Signal Travels to Phone to Make Phone Ring

Call Signal Enters the Boston Home Through Wires

Boston Picks Up the Receiver

What happens when the answerer picks up the phone's receiver?

When Boston picks up the receiver, a switch called the hook switch is released. This turns the phone "on." On modern phones, the hook switch is usually located on the base of the telephone where the receiver sits. Some phones, including most cordless models, only need the "on/off" button to be pushed to accomplish the same task.

People know a phone is on and working because they hear something in the earpiece. After answering the phone, they will hear the caller's response. If they lift the receiver to make a call, they will hear a dial tone. The tone is the sound that lets people know the telephone is connected to the local phone company.

The tone can be heard because each phone links to a supply of electricity from the phone company. Releasing the hook switch allows the electricity to flow into the base of the telephone. Once this electricity is flowing, no other calls can come through the phone line. Because the line is in use, callers trying to reach a phone that is on (off the hook) will get a different sound: a busy signal.

So how does Boston know that someone is calling?

hook switch

Little Extras

Today, telephone customers can pay extra to include special security and convenience features with their regular phone service. One example is call waiting, which eliminates busy signals. When talking on the phone and receiving another call, a listener will hear a beep when another call comes on his or her line. By pushing the hook switch or a "flash" button, the listener can switch between the two calls to tell the new caller that he or she is "on the other line."

Another option is caller identification, or caller ID. A phone call to someone with this feature travels the same way as any other call, but when it gets to the listener's phone, the phone number of the caller is displayed on a small screen.

Normally, only the phone company sees the phone numbers of callers to individual lines.

Two People
Connect by
Phone

San Diego
Hears "Hello?"

Boston says
"Hello?"

Boston Picks Up
the Receiver

Electrical Signal
Travels to
Phone to Make
Phone Ring

Call Signal
Enters the
Boston Home
Through Wires

Phone in Boston Rings

How does Boston know when to pick up the phone?

Boston knows to answer the phone because it rings. Every phone has a ringer, a device that is activated by an incoming electrical signal. The incoming signal activates a sound that announces an incoming phone call. The tone and pitch of a ringer differs with phone models—so does the process by which it is set off. Some phones use a mechanical device that strikes two bells at the same time; others use an electrical current that works with a tiny speaker. Still others have an electrical current that works with a microchip, a tiny electronic device that can produce any number of different sounds.

No matter how the ring is activated, telephones need a boost of electrical power to ring, usually an AC current of 90 volts. That is a major charge of energy, but the phone company's power supply is strong.

So how does the electrical signal get to the phone to make it ring?

Help, Emergency!

Thanks to the numbers 9-1-1, the telephone can be a lifesaver in an emergency. In most parts of United States, dialing these numbers puts the caller immediately through to the nearest emergency dispatchers. Firefighters, police, or emergency medical teams can rush to the scene of a problem within minutes of the phone call.

The 9-1-1 system was first used in 1968 when Alabama Congressman Rankin Fite placed a call from the city hall in Haleyville, Alabama, to the police station. The federal government was working with the American Telegraph & Telephone Company (the country's largest telephone company at the time)

to establish a nationwide system for reaching emergency services on the phone.

Through the late 1960s and 1970s, states adopted the 9-1-1 system in every city and county. They installed public safety answering point (PSAP) equipment in local telephone systems in order to route 9-1-1 calls through the telephone network to the nearest emergency dispatcher.

No one knows for certain why the numbers 9-1-1 were chosen. Possibly, "9" was selected because at the time no area codes began with this number. Also, "1" is the fastest number to dial on a rotary phone, and most phones back then used a rotary dial.

Two People
Connect by
Phone

San Diego
Hears "Hello?"

Boston says
"Hello?"

Boston Picks Up
the Receiver

Phone in
Boston Rings

Call Signal
Enters the
Boston Home
Through Wires

**Electrical Signal Travels to
Phone to Make Phone Ring**

What made the answerer's phone ring?

The Boston phone rings because the call, in the form of an electrical signal, comes through a wire that links the phone system in the house to the telephone. Each phone line comes into the house through one phone, and a network of wires runs from this spot to the other rooms with connected phones that have the same phone number. At each phone location, the wire goes into a plastic box called a telephone jack. The telephone plugs into the wall at the jack so electricity can flow through. A wire cord with plastic plugs at either end links the phone to the phone jack. The wires are very thin and delicate, so they are wrapped in plastic to protect them from breaking.

The typical telephone cord contains four copper wires: one colored red, one green, one yellow, and one black. Each phone line uses two of these wires to enable electrical call signals to flow to and from the phone.

So how does the electrical call signal get into the Boston house?

Make a Telephone Connection

Materials: Two telephones, 100 feet of telephone wire (available from a hardware store), one 9-volt battery, one 30-ohm resistor (available at an electronics store)

What to Do: Take a middle section of the telephone wire and strip away the plastic coating. Leave the plastic connecting plugs at either end intact. After stripping, you will see a red wire and a green wire. (Some cords have a black and yellow wire as well, but you will just use the red and green ones.) Run the red wire to the battery and a little further along to the resistor. Connect the phones at either end of the wire, using the plastic plugs. If two people pick up the phones at the same time in separate rooms, they will make a connection and be able to hear each other as clearly as if they were on a regular phone call.

Quick Questions:

1. Could you make the phones ring? Why or why not?

2. Will you hear a dial tone when you pick up one of the phones? More important, why or why not?

(Answers are on page 45)

◀ *Electricity reaches each telephone in the house through a plug in the wall called a phone jack.*

Two People
Connect by
Phone

San Diego
Hears "Hello?"

Boston says
"Hello?"

Boston Picks Up
the Receiver

Phone in
Boston Rings

Electrical Signal
Travels to
Phone to Make
Phone Ring

Call Signal Enters the Boston Home Through Wires

How did the call signal get into the Boston house?

Before the signal from San Diego goes through the Boston home's phone wiring, it arrives through a device called the *entrance bridge.* The phone company usually installs this gray plastic box in a home's basement or on an outside wall. Through a pair of copper wires, the entrance bridge links the phone wires in the Boston home to the local network of phone wires in the neighborhood.

In a city like Boston, where many people live close together, the pairs of copper wires from each phone line in a neighborhood can add up quickly. The mass of wires is braided together, or spliced, to form larger wire cables that stay protected and untangled. These sturdy cables are now often buried underground, though some are still hung from poles that reach 30 feet (10 meters) or more. The electrical call signal must first travel through this combined mass of wires to reach the Boston home.

But how does the call signal know where to go?

Telephone wires are usually run inside buildings and buried under streets in the large cities, where many people live close together.

| Signal is Programmed as Boston Phone Number | Signal Reaches Boston Neighbor-hood Through Wires and Boxes | Signal Passes Through Local Boston Exchange | Call Signal Passes Through Boston Area Exchange | Call Signal Travels Across the Country as a Light Signal | Light Signal Leaves San Diego Area Exchange | San Diego Calls the Phone Number | San Diego Picks Up the Phone |

Copper is Most Proper

Copper wire works best for sending signals without letting other forces distort the sound. With early phones, people had trouble hearing each other and they often heard crackling noises, pops, and low explosions that sounded like thunder. The sounds were caused by natural electricity in the air and on the ground. Telephone operator John J. Carty discovered that using two copper wires and twisting them together to carry the current on a telephone line would help block out these interruptions.

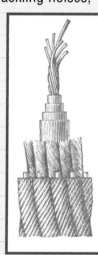

▲ Many pairs of copper wires, braided together

Signal Is Programmed as Boston Phone Number

How does the call signal know where to go?

For the electrical signal to make its way to activate the answerer's ringer, it must follow the directions contained in a set of numbers—the telephone number of the Boston home. This is the seven-digit number that connects any phone call to this particular household and no other. Phone numbers are given to customers when they open an account with the local phone company. When callers dial that number, the phone company sends the electrical call signal through the specific neighborhood to the home that has a phone with that unique phone number.

So how does the call signal know to wind up at the customer's neighborhood?

Signal Reaches Boston Neighborhood Through Wires and Boxes

Signal Passes Through Local Boston Exchange

Call Signal Passes Through Boston Area Exchange

Call Signal Travels Across the Country as a Light Signal

Light Signal Leaves San Diego Area Exchange

San Diego Calls the Phone Number

San Diego Picks Up the Phone

Multiplying Numbers

Nowadays, many households have more than one phone line. Many people need a separate phone line for in-home businesses, facsimile (fax) machines, Internet access, or talkative family members. Plus many people have cellular phones. Each new phone line means a new phone number. Since each area or city has its own particular area code—the three numbers that come before the seven-digit phone number—that can add up to a lot of phone numbers in some big cities!

Numbers can be arranged in hundreds of thousands of different combinations to create seven-digit telephone numbers. Still, some areas are actually starting to run out of phone numbers. Phone companies have solved this problem by introducing more area codes. New York City, for example, with a population of about 8 million people, now has five different area codes.

Two People
Connect by
Phone

San Diego
Hears "Hello?"

Boston says
"Hello?"

Boston Picks Up
the Receiver

Phone in
Boston Rings

Electrical Signal
Travels to
Phone to Make
Phone Ring

Call Signal
Enters the
Boston Home
Through Wires

Signal Reaches Boston Neighborhood Through Wires and Boxes

How does the call signal know to wind up in the customer's neighborhood?

As it travels through the Boston neighborhood to get to the home, the call signal from San Diego goes through a series of boxes and bunched wires. The bunches of wires start out thick, but they become increasingly thinner as they approach the single home that is the call signal's final destination.

The telephone company organizes all the wires in a neighborhood so it can find them easily to make repairs. If the wires are buried underground, repair workers can access them through small metal boxes (each about 3 feet, or 1 meter, high), which contain telephone wires for 25 to 50 homes on every block. Instead of being bound together in the box, these wires are loosely bundled so a repairperson can easily find a set of wires that is not working. These metal boxes are linked by thick cable containing many wires for hundreds of phones to larger wire stations that hold even more wires.

Before reaching the wire station, the signal passes through cables to an even larger structure that has its own power supply, an electrical station roughly the size of a park bench. This unit feeds all calls to and from the neighborhood to the local exchange. The local exchange is a building run by the telephone company to route all phone calls going in and out of the area.

But how is the information sent to the local exchange?

Telephone workers repair wires high up on telephone poles. ▶

Buried Treasures

Unlike lines that run high up on telephone poles, underground cables are not in danger of being knocked down by wind or falling trees. Buried telephone systems require digging tunnels under the ground before installing the cables. Wires are routed to metal boxes on the surface so repair workers can access them if necessary.

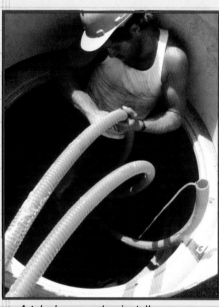

▲ *A telephone worker installs an underground cable.*

Two People
Connect by
Phone

San Diego
Hears "Hello?"

Boston says
"Hello?"

Boston Picks Up
the Receiver

Phone in
Boston Rings

Electrical Signal
Travels to
Phone to Make
Phone Ring

Call Signal
Enters the
Boston Home
Through Wires

Signal Passes Through Local Boston Exchange

How does the local exchange know where to send phone call signals?

All calls to a specific Boston neighborhood pass through the local exchange, which routes call signals going into and out of the neighborhood with the help of computers. Computers in the Boston local exchange and the other local exchanges sort call signals according to the three digits of the telephone number after the area code. These numbers generally reflect the neighborhood or town to which the call signal must be sent.

All call signals being sent to and from the local exchanges are electrical, but in order for computers at the local exchanges to understand and route a call signal, the signal must be converted to digital. Digital technology, used also in CDs and DVDs, works by storing information as a series of numbered codes. Information in digital form takes up less space than electrical signals. Digital codes can also be jumbled with other signals and then easily decoded and separated. Once the digital code is read by the computers, the signal is converted back to an electrical signal that continues to speed through wires toward its destination.

So how does the electrical call signal get to the local exchange?

Signal is Programmed as Boston Phone Number

Signal Reaches Boston Neighborhood Through Wires and Boxes

Call Signal Passes Through Boston Area Exchange

Call Signal Travels Across the Country as a Light Signal

Light Signal Leaves San Diego Area Exchange

San Diego Calls the Phone Number

San Diego Picks Up the Phone

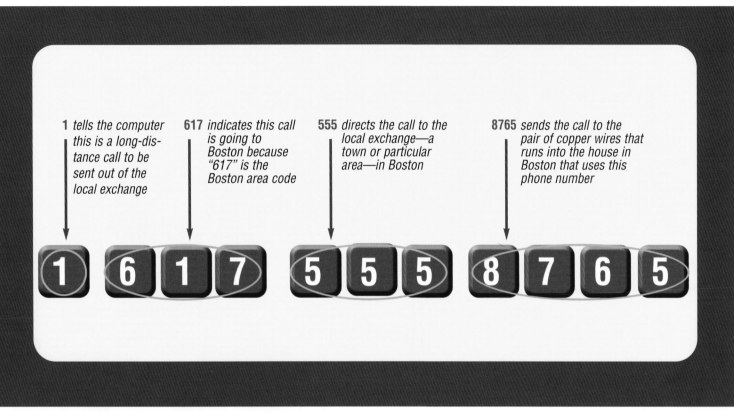

1 *tells the computer this is a long-distance call to be sent out of the local exchange*

617 *indicates this call is going to Boston because "617" is the Boston area code*

555 *directs the call to the local exchange—a town or particular area—in Boston*

8765 *sends the call to the pair of copper wires that runs into the house in Boston that uses this phone number*

1 6 1 7 5 5 5 8 7 6 5

▲ *The different parts of a telephone number*

▲ *The world's first telephone exchange, New Haven, Connecticut*

Word Spreads Fast

In 1878, only two years after the telephone was invented, the world's first local exchange opened in New Haven, Connecticut. Twenty-one customers immediately signed onto the service; within a month, the number doubled. Most customers were local businesses such as shops and drugstores.

In 1889, an undertaker in Kansas City named Almon Brown Strowger invented the first automatic exchange, an enormous machine that could connect phone calls mechanically, without a human operator. Strowger was worried that operators were listening to his conversations and sending his business to other undertakers, so he invented the machine just to take operators out of the loop! He also invented the first telephone with an automatic dialer, so the caller did not need the operator to make the phone ring on the other end.

CATCH THE WAVE

How does wireless technology, such as that used for cell phones, work?

Not all telephone calls need wires to connect to other phones. Recently, the technology to transmit telephone calls using radio waves instead of wires has developed. Radio waves are part of the *electromagnetic spectrum*, invisible waves that are constantly traveling through the air, like light and microwaves. A century ago, inventors discovered we could use these waves to send and receive information and sound.

For a telephone to pick up and send radio waves, it needs an antenna. This is a rod at the end of the telephone—just like those on portable radios. Two types of phones use this technology. One is a cordless phone, which has a handset that is not connected to the main unit by a wire; the main unit is still connected by wire to the telephone network in the house. The other portable telephone is a cellular phone, which is completely wire-free.

Cell phones use their own networks to send and receive calls. They can be used anywhere within range of a cellular base station, a structure with a large radio antenna. Calls can travel to and from this base station through a larger cellular phone exchange, which relays calls to and from cell phones in an area (just like a local telephone exchange but without wires). From there it can travel to another cellular network, if the caller is calling another cellular phone. Typically, if a cell phone caller were calling a phone on the regular ground network, the cellular exchange would convert the call from a radio signal to an electrical signal. Then it would send the call to the ground network through the wires in place to handle regular ground calls.

Up and Away

Communications satellites in space help send phone calls to and from areas that are not connected by telephone cables. They orbit the planet thousands of miles above the ground— some as high as 22,440 miles (36,112 km). Radio waves used by cellular phones do not travel very far, but satellites use microwaves to send and receive phone calls. Microwaves are shorter and more energetic than radio waves and travel at the speed of light.

▲ *A communications satellite in Earth's orbit.*

Call Signal Passes Through Boston Area Exchange

How did the call signal get to the local exchange?

Before it reached Boston's local exchange, the call signal had to pass through a series of larger telephone exchanges, including one in the city of Boston. These larger exchanges are called area exchanges.

The path of a long-distance phone call is similar to that of a train passing through different stations on its way to a final destination. Some stations are bigger than others, but all stations belong to a larger network that connects the trains to different areas. Yet unlike a train journey, a phone call travels to its destination in a matter of seconds because it is traveling at the speed of light (186,000 miles—299,330 km—per second). Just like at a local exchange, computers at the larger area exchange briefly read the call signal as a digital code before allowing it to be routed onward as an electrical call signal. In the case of the area exchange, however, the entering call signal starts out as a light signal. At the area exchange, it must be changed from a light signal to a digital signal.

So why was the call a light signal before it reached the area exchange?

San Diego

Going Global

To call someone in another country, it is necessary to dial quite a few numbers. First, the caller dials "011," which tells the network this will be an international call. After that comes the code for the country where the call is going, and then the code for the city (like our area codes). The last group of digits is the person's individual phone number.

The country code for the United States is "1." This is why even in the U.S., you must dial "1" plus the area code when making a call outside your local area.

International callers must be aware of the time zone in the areas they are calling. The globe has 24 time zones, one for each hour of the day. Going from west to east, each zone is one hour later than the previous one. The time zones start again at the international date line, which is located in the Pacific Ocean. When you cross the date line traveling east, you go back one day. So it's possible to make a phone call on Sunday that is answered halfway around the world—on Saturday!

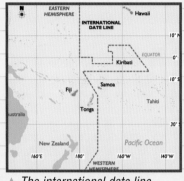

▲ The international date line

Boston

◄ A call to Boston from San Diego passes through four different time zones.

Two People Connect by Phone

San Diego Hears "Hello?"

Boston says "Hello?"

Boston Picks Up the Receiver

Phone in Boston Rings

Electrical Signal Travels to Phone to Make Phone Ring

Call Signal Enters the Boston Home Through Wires

Call Signal Travels Across the Country as a Light Signal

Why is the call a light signal?

As it travels from one coast to the other, the call signal from San Diego is passing millions of other phone calls every second. The call can travel faster and with less interference if it travels through cables as a light signal. Like radio signals, light travels in vibrating waves, but a light signal is even stronger and faster.

The signal was converted from a digital signal into a light signal at the San Diego area exchange, close to where the call originated.

So how is the signal converted to a light signal?

Ray of Light

Infrared rays are invisible to the human eye. They transmit heat and energy, like rays of visible light. Infrared rays from the sun bombard Earth all the time. Producing enough heat to cut through metal, infrared light in the form of a laser beam can be very powerful. Infrared beams are also used in remote control devices to operate TV and stereo equipment.

A technician uses infrared technology in the form of a laser beam.

Signal is
Programmed
as Boston
Phone Number

Signal Reaches
Boston Neighbor-
hood Through
Wires and Boxes

Signal Passes
Through Local
Boston Exchange

Call Signal
Passes Through
Boston Area
Exchange

Light Signal
Leaves
San Diego
Area Exchange

San Diego
Calls the
Phone Number

San Diego
Picks Up the
Phone

GLASS WORKS

How do beams of light travel without being lost or mixed with other light signals?

cladding

core

While traveling nearly at the speed of light, the lasers are contained in glass or plastic strands called *optical fibers*. Each strand is as thin as a human hair and can carry about 10,000 telephone signals at one time.

Optical fibers can carry many more phone calls than cables made of metal. Another plus is that they are thinner than copper wires, so more can be bundled together into cables. Thanks to fiber-optic technology, millions of phone conversations can take place around the world at the same time. But how can a network based on strands of glass be strong enough to do all this? Fiber-optic cables are specially made to surround and protect the fragile glass strands inside them. Each cable contains about 15 or 20 optical fibers. A plastic coating protects each strand from damage and keeps out stray light, which could interfere with the signal being carried inside. The fibers are arranged around a core of steel tubes to give the cable support. Surrounding the bundle of optical fibers and the steel core is a protective layer of tough plastic.

Although they are made of glass, optical fibers are flexible and can bend like wire. Light is able to travel through a rod that is constantly twisting and bending because each fiber is made of an inner core surrounded by an outer layer called *cladding*. The layers work together like a set of mirrors along a bending hallway: Light bounces between the core and the cladding in a process called total internal reflection.

buffer coating

How Low Do They Go?

Fiber-optic cables can lie under the ocean floor in places too deep for divers to go. Ships lay these cables using remote-operated vehicles, machines that can drop to the bottom of the sea. The vehicles bury the cables 10 feet (3 m) into the seabed to keep them safe from ocean currents and earthquakes.

▲ *Optical fibers are as thin as a human hair.*

Two People
Connect by
Phone

San Diego
Hears "Hello?"

Boston says
"Hello?"

Boston Picks Up
the Receiver

Phone in
Boston Rings

Electrical Signal
Travels to
Phone to Make
Phone Ring

Call Signal
Enters the
Boston Home
Through Wires

Light Signal Leaves San Diego Area Exchange

How is the digital signal converted to a light signal?

The signal changes form three times before it is ready to travel across the country: First, it enters the San Diego exchange as an electrical signal. Then it changes from electrical to digital. From digital it changes yet again to a light signal.

Computers at the San Diego area exchange recognize that the call is going to the city of Boston because the phone number includes the Boston area code. Understanding how far the call must travel, the computers make sure the signal that leaves the area exchange is a light signal.

The computers arrange for the call signal to travel the fastest way possible from San Diego to Boston by

| Signal is Programmed as Boston Phone Number | Signal Reaches Boston Neighborhood Through Wires and Boxes | Signal Passes Through Local Boston Exchange | Call Signal Passes Through Boston Area Exchange | Call Signal Travels Across the Country as a Light Signal | | San Diego Calls the Phone Number | San Diego Picks Up the Phone |

Phone-free Calling

Radio waves can connect people even without phones. This happens through devices called pagers, or beepers. To contact someone with a pager, the caller dials a certain telephone number, and the pager makes a beep or another signal, alerting the person that someone is trying to reach him or her. Pagers also usually display the telephone number the caller is calling from.

A pager is like a radio, except that it receives just one radio station. Each pager has its own code, called a Channel Access Protocol (CAP) code, which is linked to the telephone number that is assigned to the pager. When someone dials a particular pager's number, the signal goes to a central transmitter, which sends the signal to the pager through radio waves using the pager's CAP code.

> MEET ME AT CHELSEA MKT AT 1:00 PM FOR LUNCH

mapping out the call's path across a series of local and area exchanges between the two cities.

The call signal, however, had entered the San Diego area exchange from the local exchange as an electrical signal. At the San Diego local exchange, the call signal briefly changed to a digital code so computers there could route it. This signal leaves and enters the local San Diego exchange as an electrical signal, which was sent through wires from the caller's phone.

So how did the caller's phone send the electrical call signal?

◀ When telephones were first invented, there was no way to decode electrical signals. Therefore, a person had to connect each phone call by hand. The caller would call the local exchange and ask an operator to place a call. The operator would ring the number and connect the line on a switchboard when someone answered.

San Diego Calls the Phone Number

How did the caller's phone send the electrical call signal?

The call signal went out when the caller in San Diego called the Boston phone number. That Boston number programmed the call's electrical signals as they flowed through wires to the local exchange. Today, touch-tone calling is the most common way to make a call. The numbers are buttons, arranged in three vertical rows. Each number has its own tone, or code. A coded electrical signal is produced when the caller presses the buttons.

The call, of course, cannot happen unless the caller turns on a phone.

So how does the caller turn on the phone?

Rutherford B. Hayes

Executive Order

A telephone was installed in the White House for the first time in 1878. Then-President Rutherford B. Hayes made his first call to a man waiting only 13 miles away from the White House: Alexander Graham Bell. Reportedly, the president's first words were, "Please speak more slowly."

Signal is Programmed as Boston Phone Number

Signal Reaches Boston Neighborhood Through Wires and Boxes

Signal Passes Through Local Boston Exchange

Call Signal Passes Through Boston Area Exchange

Call Signal Travels Across the Country as a Light Signal

Light Signal Leaves San Diego Area Exchange

San Diego Picks Up the Phone

In the 1920s, all telephones used rotary dials. As the caller dialed each number and released it, the movement of the dial sent pulses to a mechanism inside the phone. The number of pulses corresponded to the numbers dialed: one pulse for the number "1," two pulses for "2," and so on. These pulses created an electrical signal that helped the local exchange route the call. ▶

Touch-tone ▶ *phones like this one produce a special tone for each number pressed.*

Two People
Connect by
Phone

San Diego
Hears "Hello?"

Boston says
"Hello?"

Boston Picks Up
the Receiver

Phone in
Boston Rings

Electrical Signal
Travels to
Phone to Make
Phone Ring

Call Signal
Enters the
Boston Home
Through Wires

San Diego Picks Up the Phone

How does the caller turn on the phone?

Like the answerer in Boston, the San Diego caller turns on the phone by lifting the receiver off the hook switch. Picking up a phone to make a call completes an electrical circuit from the phone to a computer at the local phone exchange. The dial tone the caller hears means the phone company's local exchange computers are ready to connect the caller's phone to an outside telephone line.

Operator Emergency

▲ Lowell, Massachusetts: the place where individual phone numbers began.

Telephone numbers came about partly as a result of a measles epidemic. Before 1879—just three years after Alexander Graham Bell invented the telephone—people did not have assigned telephone numbers. They called other people by dialing the operator at the local exchange first and asking him or her to direct their phone call. That year, the town of Lowell, Massachusetts, was hit with a bad case of the measles. The town doctor, Moses Greeley Parker, suggested that the town's 200 telephone owners get their own numbers. He was worried that all four of the town's operators would fall sick at the same time and the phone system would not work when people needed it most.

► *Picking up the phone completes an important electrical circuit.*

Signal is Programmed as Boston Phone Number

Signal Reaches Boston Neighborhood Through Wires and Boxes

Signal Passes Through Local Boston Exchange

Call Signal Passes Through Boston Area Exchange

Call Signal Travels Across the Country as a Light Signal

Light Signal Leaves San Diego Area Exchange

San Diego Calls the Phone Number

The Big Picture

A phone is ringing in Boston, and it is a call from San Diego. Explore the science behind answering this phone step by step:

15 Two People Connect by Phone

A person in Boston, Massachusetts, gets a phone call from San Diego, California.

(pages 6-7)

13 Boston Says "Hello?"

The mouthpiece of a phone turns sound waves into an electrical signal so the answerer can speak into the phone and have the waves travel over wires

(pages 10-11)

11 Phone in Boston Rings

The phone rings to alert the answerer that someone is calling his or her phone.

(pages 14-15)

9 Signal Enters Boston Home

The signal comes into the house through a network of copper wires in the Boston neighborhood—one pair per household.

(pages 18-19)

14 San Diego Hears "Hello?"

The earpiece of the caller's phone changes an electrical signal to sound so the caller can hear the answerer.

(pages 8-9)

12 Boston Picks Up the Receiver

The caller and answerer make a connection and conversation can start when the answerer picks up the phone receiver.

(pages 12-13)

10 Electrical Signal Makes Boston Phone Ring

An electrical signal comes through a pair of copper wires in the answerer's Boston house to make the phone ring.

(pages 16-17)

⑧ Signal Is Programmed as Boston Phone Number

The phone signal routes to the answerer's Boston home because someone dialed a particular phone number.
(pages 20-21)

⑥ Signal Reaches Boston Exchange

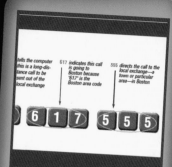

As the call passes through the Boston local telephone exchange, it briefly changes to a digital code to be understood by computers.
(pages 24-25)

④ Signal Changes from Digital to Light

The digital code turns into pulses of light beams so it can join millions of other phone signals on the fiber-optic network.
(pages 30-31)

② San Diego Calls the Phone Number

The caller sends the phone call on its journey by punching in the Boston telephone number, which sends out an electrical signal.
(pages 36-37)

⑦ Signal Reaches Boston Neighborhood

The Boston home's copper wires get bundled up with many other wires outside the home and stretch to the local exchange.
(pages 22-23)

⑤ Signal Passes Through Area Exchange

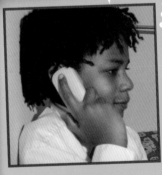

The call comes into Boston through the Boston area exchange. Computers arrange the fastest route from the local exchange in San Diego.
(pages 28-29)

③ Signal Changes from Electric to Digital

The call comes into Boston through the Boston area exchange. Computers arrange the fastest route from the local exchange in San Diego.
(pages 34-35)

① San Diego Picks Up the Phone

To make a call to Boston, the caller in San Diego first picks up the phone to turn it on and hears the dial tone.
(pages 38-39)

Take a tour of the telephone industry through time.

Growing and Growing

The phone industry in the United States gets bigger every year. Here is a quick look at how things have changed.

- In 1920, only 35 percent of households had telephones. Today, it is 95 percent, or about 102 million households.

- Cellular phones first hit the market in Chicago in 1983. People considered them a business luxury. By the next year, about 92,000 Americans were using cellular phones. By 2001, this figure jumped to 118 million.

- Americans are making more calls to other countries. In 1980, more than 200 million international calls were placed. Twenty years later, in 2000, the total was 6.6 billion.

- More and more homes are getting second lines. In 1980, about 3 percent of U.S. households had second lines. Today, that figure is about 27 percent and growing.

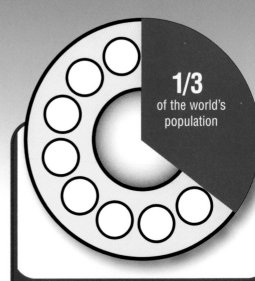

1/3 of the world's population

Not Phony

Phone use is growing in the United States, but not everywhere in the world. One-third of the world's population—about 2 billion people—have never had the chance to use a telephone.

Paying Your Way

Public phones—coin-operated phones found in public buildings, gas stations, airports, at bus stops, on street corners, and other places—are slowly becoming less common, perhaps because cell phones have become more popular. The total number of pay phones in America decreased by 200,000 between 1999 and 2001.

Pay phones have a long history. The first was installed in 1889 at a bank in Hartford, Connecticut. Many public phones at that time used special tokens instead of regular coins.

Inventing the Telephone: A Timeline

1876: Alexander Graham Bell says the first words through a telephone.

1877: Thomas Edison improves on the telephone with his invention of a carbon-based microphone.

1878: The first telephone exchange opens for business in New Haven, Connecticut.

1889: Almon Brown Strowger invents the automatic exchange and the dial telephone.

1892: By calling Chicago from New York, Bell places the first long-distance call.

1919: Replacing the human operator, the automatic switchboard is widely introduced to the phone system.

Telephones Through Time

The telephone has changed a lot since it got its start in 1876.

1880s	1910s	1920s	1930s
The caller had to stand right next to the phone to speak into the mouthpiece. The hand crank made the phone ring on the other end.	The earpiece stayed the same, but the main part of the phone was freestanding.	Wider use of automatic exchanges meant people could dial calls directly.	Phones were easier to handle once the mouthpiece and earpiece were joined in the handset.

1960s	1980s	2000	2002 and beyond
As fashions changed, so did the shapes and sizes of phones.	Thanks to cordless technology, people could talk without having to sit right next to the phone.	For cellular phones, the smaller and lighter the cellular phone, the better.	It will not be long before we will routinely be able to see the person we are talking to.

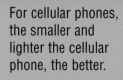

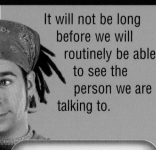

▶ **Real Estate Appraisers**

Wonders and Words

Explore some common questions and misconceptions about how phones work.

Q: *Will telephones still work if the electricity goes out?*

A: Telephones will work because they get their power supply from the phone company, not the electric company. But cordless and cellular phones will only work for a limited time: They both use batteries that need to be recharged from a main unit plugged into the wall. Once the battery runs out of power, the phone will not work until the electricity in the house comes back on.

Q: *Can one telephone ring to different numbers?*

A: Yes. A phone can be unplugged and moved to another phone line or even to another house, and it will ring if someone dials the phone number for that line.

Q: *Will old phones from the 1920s and 1930s work on a modern telephone network?*

A: Yes, all that is needed is a working phone line. Even though the phone network has been updated with computers and fiber-optic technology, it still ends in each household with a pair of copper wires. Almost from the time they were first invented, telephones have used copper wires to send and receive sound.

Q: *Why do movies and books use phone numbers with an exchange of "555"?*

A: The numbers "555" belong to a telephone exchange that does not exist. If a person tries to dial a number with that exchange, the call will not go through. Movies use fake phone numbers so audiences will not be tempted to bother people by dialing real phone numbers they see or hear.

Q: *How can the phone be used in emergencies?*

A: The numbers "911" will automatically connect the caller to an operator who works with the police, the fire department, and emergency medical services. Emergency workers respond to a 911 call within minutes.

Q: *Can people with impaired hearing use the phone?*

A: Yes, with special types of phones. Some phones are amplified so the caller's voice comes through louder in the earpiece. Another helpful machine is a teletypewriter, or TTY. This has a keyboard and a display screen, so the caller can type a message instead of speaking, and can read the other person's response in the screen.

Glossary

Area exchange: The telephone facility that handles all long-distance calls in that area code

Dial tone: The sound provided by the phone company that lets the caller know the line is working before making a phone call

Entrance bridge: A plastic box, usually located in a home's basement or on an outside wall, that acts as a bridge between a phone and the network of telephone wire in a neighborhood

Diaphragm: A flexible disk inside a telephone earpiece and mouthpiece that bends to sound vibrations

Digital: A code based on switching between two digits, "0" and "1"

Earpiece: The speaker part of the phone used to hear the caller's voice

Hook switch: A telephone's "on and off" switch, usually located on the handset

Infrared: Electromagnetic radiation that is invisible to the human eye

Keypad: Touch-sensitive pad on top of the phone that is electronically connected through wires

Laser: A high intensity beam of light

Local exchange: The telephone facility that sends and receives all calls in a particular region

Mouthpiece: The microphone part of the phone, which the caller speaks into

Optical fibers: Glass or plastic strands that carry light signals

Receiver: The handset part of a telephone containing the earpiece and mouthpiece

Sound wave: A vibration in the air caused by sound

Switchboard: The panel in a local telephone exchange that receives and connects phone calls

Answer to Brain Teasers from Page 17

1. *The phones will not ring because you will not have enough power from the 9-volt battery to activate the ringers.*
2. *You would not hear the dial tone because you are not connected to the phone company's electricity supply.*

Index

Credits:

Produced by: J. A. Ball Associates, Inc.
Jacqueline Ball, Justine Ciovacco
Daniel H. Franck, Ph.D., Science Consultant

Art Direction, Design, and Production:
designlabnyc
Todd Cooper, Sonia Gauba

Writer: Lelia Mander

Cover: Brooke Fasani: girl on telephone, dialing phone (bottom right); Ablestock/Hemera: phone wires, fiber optic cable; PhotoDisc, Inc.: telephone worker on pole.

Interior: Jim Wildeman Studio: p.9, telephone, p.10, telephone; Brooke Fasani: p.7 girl on telephone, p.13 hook switch, p.26 boy on telephone, p.28 boy, p.29, girl, p.37 dialing the phone; Sonia Gauba: p.13 caller ID, p.25 telephone number, p.32 diagram, p.35 pager; Photospin: p.6 drain, p.21 water tank, lower left, p.31 reservoir, p.36 snowstorm, p.39 camel, p.42 snow on mountain, p.43 astronaut, tape measure, water, p.44 toilet, bottle; PhotoDisc, Inc.: p.22 telephone worker on pole, p.23 telephone worker in hole, p.27 satellite, p.33 fiber optic cable, p.27: boy with toothbrush, p.37 puddle, p.48 water drops; Library of Congress: p.11 crank telephone, p.25 New Haven, p.36 Rutherford B. Hayes, p.38 Lowell, Massachusetts, p.43 Alexander Graham Bell; Ablestock/Hemera: p.15 green telephone, antique telephone, p.19 city, p.20 office telephone, woman on telephone, fax machine, woman on telephone, man using computer, p.30 television and remote control, p.37 rotary dial, p.39 hanging up, p.42 boy, girl, telephone off hook, p.43 pay telephone, antique telephones; ArtToday.com: p.19 copper coil; Photospin.com: p.21 pay telephone, p.43 quarters; ©PhotoResearchers, Inc.: p.31 man with fiber optic cable; ©Bettmann/CORBIS: telephone operators.

For More Information

Berger, Melvin and Gilda. *Telephones, Televisions, and Toilets: How They Work (and What Can Go Wrong).* New York: Chelsea House, 1998.

Bender, Lionel. *Eyewitness Books: Invention.* New York: Alfred A. Knopf, 1991.

Gearhart, Sarah. *Turning Point Inventions: The Telephone.* New York: Athenaeum Books for Young Readers, 1999.

Macaulay, David. *The Way Things Work.* Boston: Houghton Mifflin, 1988.

Parker, Steve. *53 1/2 Things That Changed the World.* Brookfield, Conn.: The Millbrook Press, 1992.

www.howstuffworks.com Interesting, easy-to-understand information on science, electronics, entertainment, trends, style, and more.